A DAY AT A TIME

Other Books by
DENIS DUNCAN

As Author

CREATIVE SILENCE
Through Inner Silence to the Harvest of the Spirit
(*Amulree Paperback No. 1, Arthur James, Evesham*)

HERE IS MY HAND
The story of the remarkable ministry of Salvation Army
officer, Colonel Alida Bosshardt and her twenty-seven
year service in the 'Red Light' district of Amsterdam
(*Hodder and Stoughton*)

As Editor, with Introductions

Through the Year with William Barclay (now in
paperback)
Through the Year with Cardinal Heenan
Through the Year with J. B. Phillips
Every Day with William Barclay (now in paperback)
Marching Orders (William Barclay for younger readers,
paperback)
Marching On (William Barclay for younger readers,
paperback)
(*all Hodder and Stoughton*)

In the USA only

Daily Celebration, Volumes I and II
J. B. Phillips for this Day (Bantam Books)
(*all Word Books Inc. Waco, Texas*)
Marching Orders
Marching On
(*Westminster Press, Philadelphia, Pennsylvania*)

In Japan only

Through the Year with William Barclay, Every Day with
William Barclay, Marching Orders and Marching On are
published in Japanese by the Jordan Press, Tokyo.

A DAY AT A TIME

A Thought and a Prayer
for Each Day of the Year

by
DENIS DUNCAN

Part I: July–December

Amulree Paperback No. 2
published by
ARTHUR JAMES LIMITED
The Drift, Evesham,
Worcs., England

First Edition 1980

© Denis Duncan

All rights reserved by the publishers
Arthur James Limited of Evesham, Worcs., England

DUNCAN, DENIS
A day at a time.
Part 1: July - December
1. Devotional calendars
I. Title
242'.2   BV4810
ISBN 0-85305-223-9

Printed by **Gibbons Barford** Wolverhampton

PREFACE

I offer "a thought and a prayer" for each day of a year in the hope that they will provide encouragement, strength and healing to those who receive them. The "thoughts" are drawn – by permission of the Editor of Christian Weekly Newspapers (146 Queen Victoria Street, London EC4) – from my weekly devotional half-page in *British Weekly*, both from the main series of articles and from my diary column "A Day at a Time". I have also drawn on other areas of my writing, including *Here is my Hand*, the story of the famous Salvation Army officer, Colonel Alida Bosshardt, who ministered for 27 years in the so-called 'Red Light' area of Amsterdam. It is published by Hodder & Stoughton (1977). The prayers include my "Saturday Prayers" in the *British Weekly* column, but the majority of the prayers appear for the first time here.

I hope readers will simply begin on the day on which they discover the book and go through the year from there! Perhaps some thoughts will strike a chord or stimulate reflection. I hope the prayers will minister to inner healing and forward the processes of integration through the Spirit.

If inadvertently an acknowledgement has not been made – for over periods of time one gathers material for use in speaking and preaching without always recording the source – I would be glad to hear about the omission and take the first opportunity available to repair it.

In the prayers, I have, after consideration, decided to use "You" rather than "Thou". I know some would prefer the more traditional form, but I have felt the form I have chosen "fits" the ethos of these particular prayers.

The present volume covers July to December. Volume 2 will appear later in the year, ready for January to June.

As always, I record my deep appreciation of the consistent, capable and caring work of Jillian Tallon in typing the manuscript.

I hope sincerely that some of these thoughts and prayers will help somebody, somewhere. If so, the work has been justified.

DENIS DUNCAN

CONTENTS

Firm Foundations

July 1

A Thought

These are three benedictions in Psalm 84:

Blessed is the one whose Joy is in God (verses 1–4)
Blessed is the one whose Strength is in God (verses 5–8)
Blessed is the one whose Trust is in God (verses 9–12)

Joy, Strength and Trust "in God" make for true inner Peace.

A Prayer

Grant me, O Lord
  Time for Thought
  Space for Solitude
  Room for Reflection
  and a Place for Prayer
So may I be renewed daily
  Through Jesus Christ, our Lord

                    Amen

July 2

A Thought

How often Jesus uses the word "must" – of what He has to do.

"I *must* be about my Father's business" (Luke 2:49)
"I *must* preach the Kingdom of God" (Luke 4:43)
"I *must* work the works of Him that sent me" (John 9:4)
"Them also I *must* bring" (John 10:16)
"Today I *must* abide at thy house" (Luke 19:5)
"The Son of man *must* be lifted up" (John 12:34)

The pressure that comes in the word "must", in each case, had to do with the will of God. Treat with respect an inner sense that says "you must". It involves conviction   *and* commitment for *you*.

A Prayer

I bless You, O Lord, for
    New mercies given
    Old weaknesses accepted
    Fresh opportunities offered
    Love, unchanging, received

Help me always, in grateful response, to press toward the mark for the prize of the high calling of God in Christ Jesus
                        Amen

July 3

A Thought

Are you depressed by temptation, overwhelmed with failure, despondent over growth in grace? Be comforted. Father Andrew reminds us of the universality of such feelings in *In the Silence.* "It is the testimony of all the saints from the beginning," he writes, "that the spiritual life is a combat." It is – but we are never left to battle alone.

A Prayer

In the mysteries of life, O Lord
    Grant us
        Infinite trust
        Calm confidence
        Profound insight
        Inexhaustible hope

Then may we find that, loving You, all things do truly work together for good
                        Amen

July 4

A Thought

Three gardens of the Bible speak to us –
    Eden, the Garden of Creation
    Gethsemane, the Garden of Dereliction
    The Garden of the Resurrection

Life *is* Creation, Dereliction and Resurrection – together.

A Prayer

Forgive my "foolish ways". O God
  and make me wise
If "fool" I must be
  let it be only "for Christ's sake"
And in such "foolishness"
  may Yours be the glory

Amen

July 5

A Thought

Do not worry if growth in grace is slow. "We should be the 'waiting ones' ", writes Sister Eva of Friedenshort. "The 'work of transfiguration' is one that goes forward gradually".

A Prayer

Looking back, may I be filled with gratitude
Looking forward, may I be filled with hope
Looking upward, may I be conscious of strength
Looking inward, may I find deep peace

Amen

July 6

A Thought

There is a marvellous statement by the great preacher P. T. Forsyth. He writes:

"I should count a life well spent, and the world well lost, if after tasting all its experiences and facing all its problems, I had no more to show, at its close, or to carry to another life, than the acquisition of a real, sure, humble and grateful faith in the eternal and incarnate Son of God."

A Prayer
Peace be with me
   awake
   asleep
   by day in toil
   by night in rest
Peace be with me
   always
                                    Amen

July 7

A Thought

"This is the business of our life
   By effort and toil
   By prayer and supplication
   To advance in the Grace of God"
So wrote St. Augustine.

A Prayer
Let the note of joy
   be in my undertakings
Let the note of faith
   be in my living
Let the note of hope
   be in my dying
Let the gift of peace
   be always with me
                                    Amen

July 8

A Thought

   Meddling with the psychic is not profitable, but a deep
involvement with that more profound dimension – the
spiritual – is. Only as we are in touch with the spiritual and
affected by it, can we reach both the profundity of the faith
and the harvest that follows from such contact. It is in the
deep places that we meet God.

A Prayer

Take me, O Lord
*   to where I shall meet with You*
Lead me, O Lord
*   in ways of holiness and righteousness*
Guide me, O Lord
*   to the hidden springs of faith*
Bring me, O Lord
*   to knowledge of the Truth in Christ Jesus*
So may I have a happy journey's end

Amen

July 9

A Thought

Look to the day for its life
   the very life of life
In its brief course lie all its realities
   and truths of existence –
      The joy of growth
      The splendour of action
      The glory of power
For yesterday is but a memory
   and tomorrow is only a vision
But today, well-lived, makes every
   yesterday a memory of happiness
   and every tomorrow a vision of life
Look well therefore to this day.
So runs an ancient Sanskrit poem.

A Prayer

Make this day, O Lord, a day
*   of generous giving*
*   and gracious receiving*
*   of blessings offered*
*   and blessings added*

of joy outflowing
    and joy experienced
So may the day end
    with deep peace and satisfaction

                        Amen

July 10

A Thought

We are – as Rod McKuen reminds us – "Children one and all". Child-like qualities (as distinct from childishness) will be, not our shame, but our joy for "except you become as a little child, you cannot enter the Kingdom of God". There is a "holy innocence" which is an attribute of true faith. God grant us the child-like heart!

A Prayer
Help me, O Lord
    to be child-like
        in simple trust
        in holy innocence
        in spontaneous intuition
        in acceptance of miracle
So may I more nearly
    enter Your Kingdom

                        Amen

July 11

A Thought

There are two phrases in William Barclay's rendering of the first letter of Peter that are quite memorable. First he speaks of Christians as "exiles of eternity" and sums up beautifully just where our abiding home is. Then he describes disciples as those "who are travelling on the road to holiness in the power of the Spirit".

What a pilgrimage!

A Prayer
You are, O God, the
  rest of the weary
  joy of the sad
  hope of the dreary
  light of the glad
May rest and joy and hope and light
  be Your gifts to me

                    Amen

July 12

A Thought

It is acknowledgement, not attainment, that leads to life. It is the act of receiving, not the fact of deserving that restores relationship. This is the Gospel, the Good News to sorely troubled souls, who seek inner peace. It is not in the strain and stress of the spiritual struggle against the odds, nor is it in the need to please, to satisfy "the Divine potentate", that salvation lies. It lies in the acceptance of a gift.

A Prayer

Let joy be natural to me, O Lord
  so that I uplift others
Let enthusiasm never die within me, O Lord
  so that I inspire others
Let enterprise be my mark, O Lord
  so that I contribute to Divine surprises
Let peace be my gift, O Lord
  so that I add to the peace of others

                    Amen

July 13

A Thought

In the parish church at Long Melford in Suffolk, England, there is the famous Rabbit window, depicting three rabbits.

Each has two ears, but there are only three between them. The guide-book suggests that this is a symbol of the Trinity.

The doctrine of the Trinity is a word-mystery, but the doctrine itself is an expression, in theological terms, of our human experience of the one God who comes to us in three ways – as Father, Christ and in the Holy Spirit. Yet there is and can be only one God.

The doctrine is a statement of what Christians know, by faith, to be reality.

A Prayer
My mind is too small, O God
  to comprehend Your greatness
But I feel Your presence
  every passing hour
So I rest in peace
  then go my way

                    Amen

July 14

A Thought

It is worth remembering at the beginning or end of each day Teilhard de Chardin's familiar words: "All that really matters is devotion to something bigger than ourselves".

A Prayer
Holy, holy, holy
  Lord God Almighty
Heaven and earth are
  full of Your Glory
I praise You, O God
  I acknowledge You to be my Lord
And with all the earth
  I worship You
    Father everlasting

                    Amen

July 15

A Thought

The witness of the Bible in its entirety is to a relationship damaged by the sin of man in the beginning and to the possibility of relationship restored in the fullness of time. That witness includes consistent emphasis on the inability of man, on his own initiative or by his own effort, to make good the damage done through his pride, wilfulness and arrogance. That same witness points in only one direction – to the divine solution. "By grace you are saved through faith."

A Prayer
You are "the Lord of all being, throned afar"
  Yet to each loving heart,
    You are so near
You are the Creator of heaven and earth
  Yet to each child of God
    You are "Our Father"
Thanks be to You, O God
  for Your greatness
    and Your nearness

                    Amen

July 16

A Thought

Jesus Christ is the same yesterday, today and for ever. The pre-existent Christ ("in the beginning was the Word") is Jesus of Nazareth who is "my beloved Son", who died and rose again. The whole purpose of the "Divine plan of salvation " is to restore humanity to the wholeness God seeks for all – which is one-ness with Himself, through Christ, in the Spirit. Integration is "through the Spirit".

A Prayer
When I am overwhelmed
  with darkness
      depression
        defeat
Lift my eyes
  my heart
    my soul
to the One "lifted up" for me
Then may I be made new

                    Amen

July 17

A Thought

When Henry Drummond was unorthodox and
theologically suspect, the great evangelist Sankey, whom he
knew, asked where he stood. Drummond replied in memorable words, which he emphasised were *his* words and *his*
deepest convictions:

"The power to set the heart right, to renew the springs of
affection, comes from Christ. The sense of the infinite
worth of a single soul, and the recoverableness of man at
his worst are the gifts of Christ. The freedom from guilt,
the forgiveness of sins, comes from Christ's Cross: the
hope of immortality springs from Christ's grave . . ."

A Prayer
Come Holy Spirit, come
  cleanse me, so that I may be more holy
Fill me with new life
  breathe into me new power
And make my heart truly
  Your home

                    Amen

July 18

A Thought

Despite the violence and the vilification, the mobs and the murders, the robberies and the rapes, the wars and the rumours of wars, never let us forget the wonders of this amazing world − the beauty of the earth, the glories of the skies, the creative possibilities in the arts, science and technology, the gladness of children, the glory of so many people, the consistency of nature and the grace revealed, within the world, in Jesus. *How lovely* − despite so much − *is our dwelling-place!*

A Prayer

I stand before Your cross, O Lord, in wonder
"There was no other good enough,
  to pay the price of sin"
Prevent me, O Lord, from
  "crucifying You afresh"
Redeem me from that which
  adds to Your pain
Then may I serve You only as You deserve

                              Amen

July 19

A Thought

Who is this Man that even the winds and sea obey Him? (Matthew 8:27). What is the origin of the "authority" with which He speaks? The answer is in Peter's historic, intuitive summing-up of all that he had come to believe: "Thou art the Christ, the Son of the living God" (Matthew 16:16).

Christ's "mastery" is rooted in His divinity. "You call me Master and Lord . . . and so I am" (John 13:13). The Gospels therefore present Jesus as Master over disease, evil spirits and, ultimately, over death. It is in this capacity that He helps us.

A Prayer

O Master, let me walk
  in Your company
    hearing Your words
    seeing Your deeds
    feeling Your love
And having walked with You
  along the road of life
May I walk with others
  in Your name

                              Amen

July 20

A Thought

"Who will rescue me from this body which turns life into death?" asks Paul (Romans 7:24, William Barclay). The answer he gives himself (verse 25): "God alone can through Jesus Christ our Lord. Thanks be to Him!"

A Prayer

Help me, O God
  to have
    a sense of humour
    a sense of fun
    an ability to laugh
  to use it
    never hurtfully
    always generously

                              Amen

July 21

A Thought

The secret of the life that is to be abundant is the reservoir of peace built into our wholeness; a reservoir that, if fed by the activity of the Divine Spirit, need never be exhausted.

A Prayer
Let the breath of the Spirit
* fall on me*
Let the energy of the Spirit
* come into me*
So may I be transformed and inspired
* to serve Your cause today*

Amen

July 22

A Thought

We cannot move towards health or wholeness if we neglect the growth of the *spiritual* part of our beings. Any philosophy of life that fails to acknowledge this truth, is, in the words of the old evangelical hymn, a "broken cistern". The salvation of the soul, the attainment of wholeness, integration – call it what you will – involves Christ at the centre and growth through the Spirit. This is the truth about life.

A Prayer
Let my love be without pretence
* May I abhor that which is evil*
*   Make me cleave to that which is good*
All through the Christ who dwells within me

Amen

July 23

A Thought

If there is one passage in which the *New English Bible* translators have surpassed themselves, it must be the section Ephesians 3:14–21. There is hardly a word in it that does not lead to the things of the Spirit. Just take a part of it each day for a week and think on these words:

"I kneel in prayer to the Father, from whom every family in heaven and on earth takes its name, that out of the treasures of his glory, he may grant you strength and power through his Spirit in your inner being."

The "treasures of his glory". "Strength and Power". "Through his Spirit". "In your inner being".

What a prayer!

A Prayer
"Hallowed by Thy Name!"
This loving reverence I offer
in Jesu's name

Amen

July 24

A Thought

"That through faith, Christ may dwell in your hearts in love."

How central to Paul is "faith", the soul's response to the gift of Christ. To be "in Christ", to have Christ in you, is the goal of discipleship. It is possible – but by faith alone.

A Prayer

Help me, O Lord
to know whom I have believed
to be persuaded that You are able to do that
which I have committed to You
Then shall I rest in peace
knowing that it is not my grasp of You
but Your grasp of me
that is important

Amen

July 25

A Thought

"With deep roots . . ."

Roots, the growing tree, reaching heavenwards, but spreading its branches outwards too. It is so like the Christian personality – rooted in personal history and culture, growing heavenwards – towards Christ, reaching outwards – in community responsibility. So we become "the leaves of the tree" that are for "the healing of the nations".

A Prayer

Make quiet my mind and heart
  for the inflow of God's Spirit
Illumine me with the Light of the world
Fill me with the Peace that passes all understanding
So there shall flow out of me to all
  Light and Peace and Love
                              Amen

July 26

A Thought

"... and firm foundations". How rock-like it feels! How secure, Jesus said in the Sermon on the Mount, is "the house built on rock". How natural the Church should be built around Peter, "the rock". "For other foundation can no man lay than that is laid, which is Jesus Christ" (I Cor. 3:11). "That Rock was Christ" (I Cor. 10:4).

A firm foundation.

A Prayer

Lord, keep me safe this night
  secure from all my fears
May angels guard me while I sleep
  till morning light appears
                              Amen

July 27

A Thought

  "With deep roots and firm foundations, may you be strong

to grasp, with all God's people, what is the breadth, length, depth and height of the love of Christ." Salvation is the gift of God! We do not have to earn it, deserve it, merit it, work for it. Just receive it! So let there be no tentative feeling-out: grasp it, take it, hold it, receive it. It is there – for all.

A Prayer
Amid life's storms, make me still
Amid life's changes, make me strong
If criticism comes, keep me steadfast
If sadness comes, keep me brave
   Make my weakness strong
   through the grace that is sufficient for me

Amen

July 28

A Thought

   "Grasp the love of Christ and know it, though it is beyond knowledge." What a paradox is in these words! A knowledge which is beyond knowledge! For the knowledge that comes in faith is another kind of knowledge. It is not subject to logic, rationality, proof. It is intuitional knowledge – or as Paul says to the Galatians, "by direct revelation".

   We know Christ's love through that kind of knowledge.

A Prayer
Still the waves
Quieten the storms
Hold the tiller in your hand
Fill the sails with the wind of the Spirit
So may I reach the desired haven
And drop anchor in Your love

Amen

July 29

A Thought

"Now to Him who is able to do *immeasurably more* than all we can ask or conceive..." That phrase "immeasurably more" sums up the vast difference between finite, human understanding and the infinite, Divine understanding. Our faith is not in the "most" we can understand but in the "more" of the Divine unlimitedness.

A Prayer

Grant to me, O Lord
Eyes to see the beauty of the world
and the inner eye to discern the wonder of the Spirit
Ears to hear the sounds of nature
and the inner ear to hear the music of the spheres
Hands to help me work and play and love
and hands of use to the Spirit for the healing of mankind

Amen

July 30

A Thought

"So may you attain to fullness of being, the fullness of God Himself." The way to wholeness is through the way of Christ – in all its wonder. So faith alone is the way to fullness.

A Prayer

May the Light that shone in Christ, my Lord
illumine my heart
May that same Light
shine down the road that lies ahead of me
And suffuse my path with its radiance

Amen

July 31

A Thought

Apa Pant, the distinguished Indian writer and statesman, in his book *A Moment of Time*, tells of his "journey of discovery", a journey for his soul. He says the journey would have been impossible but for the "profound and powerful, constant and most loving, kind and at the same time challenging and demanding Presence that came to me as a privilege of life".

A Prayer
Help me, O Lord, to see in moments of time, not merely coincidence, but the surprises of the Spirit
So may I live each day, conscious of Your Providence and aware of Your Presence in the significant "moments of time", prepared for me
Through Jesus Christ, our Lord

Amen

When all is dark . . .

August 1

A Thought

The text for the Divine Sensitivity is that "He knows our needs before we ask". The text for the Divine Empathy is that "He suffered and was tempted . . . like as we are".

A Prayer

Make me conscious, O Lord
of the church militant of which I am a part
Make me conscious, O Lord
of the church triumphant by which I am encompassed
May my awareness of
the communion of Your saints be an encouragement to me
Through Jesus Christ, our Lord

Amen

August 2

A Thought

"Man's extremity is God's opportunity." How true these words feel when I walk through the valley of the shadows. "He descended into hell." How real these words feel when I look at the depths from which people need lifting. But it is not "man's extremity" that is decisive. It is the way God grasps the opportunity "whereby we may be saved".

For the God who acts so, let us give thanks.

A Prayer

All our hope is founded
on You, O God
You forgive our iniquities
You heal our diseases
You crown us with loving-kindness and mercy
You redeem our lives from destruction
Our hope is surely placed

Amen

August 3

A Thought

There is no way to the healing of the memories that does not pass through the facing of the memories, the acknowledgement of the memories, the acceptance of the memories and the redemption of the memories. The road to resurrection goes via Calvary.

Per ardua ad astra is true in the life of the Spirit, too. It *is* through hurt and hardship we reach the stars.

A Prayer
Let remembrances of my failure, O Lord
*   not be a wallowing in what I have failed to be and do*
Let it rather lead me to
*   the rock that is higher than I*
*   the grace which is all-sufficient*
*   the love that is all-forgiving*
So may my failures be the
*   place where victory begins*

                              Amen

August 4

A Thought

"A weak faith," writes Viktor Frankl (in *The Unconscious God*) "is weakened by predicaments and catastrophes whereas a strong faith is strengthened by them." The suffering saints have shown this again and again—to God's glory and our strengthening.

A Prayer
Send, O Lord
*   Your ministering angels*
*   silently, to enfold us*
*   subtly, to strengthen us*

sensitively, to encourage us
spontaneously, to surprise us
May the angels who came to minister to You, O Lord
bring their blessings to Your people

Amen

August 5

A Thought

That well-known declaration by a young Jew on the
wall of a Warsaw ghetto never fails to move and stir:
"I believe in the sun even if it does not shine
I believe in love even though I do not feel it
I believe in God even if I do not see Him".

A Prayer

Bless us with friends, O Lord
and bless them through us
Bless us when we have to stand alone
and bear the pain only we can bear
Bless us through the Divine Friendship
which comes when "other helpers fail"
"O Thou who changest not
Abide with me"

Amen

August 6

A Thought

Jesus' Gethsemane cry: "Thy will, not mine be done" is
about faith's triumph over total disillusionment. The miracle
of deliverance from suffering, as Jesus knows, is not to
happen, but the greater miracle of resurrection is—and it did.

A Prayer

Keep me
  trusting in You, O God
  looking towards You, O Christ
  walking with You, O Holy Spirit
So may I have grace
  Thrice over

Amen

August 7

A Thought

There are many in the Garden of Gethsemane and we must pray for them.

A Prayer

O Lord,
  make me understanding
    of all that is around me
    accepting that which is good and lovely
    rejecting all that corrupts and destroys
    aware of all that you can redeem
    both outside me and inside me

Amen

August 8

A Thought

We all have a right to our secrets, but to hold things back from God is pointless, for (I repeat) "He knows before we ask". Do not hold back honest recognition of your negative or "shadow" side either. We need to know and accept ourselves, "warts and all", in order to make our most creative contributions to life.

A Prayer

When I fail greatly
  lift me up
When I am arrogant
  put me down
When I love greatly
  give me joy
When I am loved greatly
  grant me peace
When love is taken away
  let me not be bitter
When love returns
  make me glad
When all seems lost
  support me
When all is well
  make me grateful

Amen

August 9

A Thought

Rejection, loneliness, desolation—all are parts of experience, and can feel like a load that is too heavy to be borne. But if the sense of rejection can be reduced and the sense of the never-rejecting God created; if loneliness can be lightened; if a tiny flower begins to bloom in the desert places, the day has not been in vain.

A Prayer

Make us conscious, O Lord
  of the infinite variety and diversity of Your world
  its cultures and its customs
  its many highways to truth
  its many ways of worship
And having seen such diversities of gifts

May we know
  the presence of one Holy Spirit
  the gift of one cosmic Christ who is the Son of the one God
  and Father of us all

Amen

August 10

A Thought

It is hard to believe "He holds the whole world in His hands" sometimes. War, violence, bombs, prejudice—the denial of His presence is so prevalent. But crucifixion precedes resurrection, while the hate of Calvary is the doorway to the resurrection of Love. The darkest hour *is* just before the dawn.

A Prayer
May I always know, O Lord, that all depends
  Not on my grasp of You
  But on Your grasp of me
Then will all be truly well

Amen

August 11

A Thought

We find it easy to quote Paul's words: "All things work together for good" but often forget to complete the quotation which says "to them that love God". The qualification is important.

A Prayer
Grant, O Lord, that I may see Your hand
  in the way things work together for good
Grant, that, so seeing, I may want to
  love You more

And in the happenings of the Spirit
  may I see Your Love

Amen

August 12

A Thought

"Ought not Christ to have suffered these things?" asked
the Stranger on the road to Emmaus. When those who are
suffering deeply can see a shaft of light on the meaning of
suffering that these words bring, the effect on "total" health is
remarkable. But it is only those who are in deep suffering who
can pay tribute to such truth. On the lips of those for whom
all seems to be going well, it sounds so glib.

A Prayer
How hard it is, O Lord
  to see You in the suffering
    of so many
But the suffering which was Yours
  has shed a light that illumines my way
  and so leads me to greater understanding
Bless that which I have learned through suffering

Amen

August 13

A Thought

I have twice learned, painfully, the danger of ignoring the
inner pressure to do something. On both occasions, I did not
go quickly enough to see two great churchmen, men of the
Spirit, before they died in the prime of their lives. There was
not time—but there ought to have been time, as I know now.
Remembering George Gunn and Tom Allan, I try never to
make that mistake of omission again. I do not know what
they thought I could give them. I know what I missed.

A Prayer

O Lord, make me quick
  to hear
    to answer
      to minister
  make me aware of
    the smallest and most still voice within
      calling me to Your work
May I say with Samuel:
  "Speak, Lord, I hear"
    with Isaiah
      "Here am I, send me!"

                    Amen

August 14

A Thought

Carlo Carretto is well-known as a profoundly spiritual soul. But he has as saints do (but are not always seen to have) a very practical side. He is helpful when he writes "Don't keep saying 'everything has collapsed already!' You will find it much more cheering and rewarding to think of yourself as building for a new tomorrow, than as defending a past already old."

A Prayer

When everything is against me
  Grant me the will to strive
When everyone is against me
  Grant me the will to live
When all I have is threatened
  Grant me the strength to be

                    Amen

August 15

A Thought

Harry Williams in his book, *Tensions*, tells us that, in Jewish Rabbinic thought, man is said to have a Good Inclination and an Evil Inclination. In the Shema ("Thou shalt love the Lord thy God with all Thy heart", etc.) the Hebrew word for "heart" occurs in the form spelt with two *beths*, so many rabbis interpreted this as indicating that man is to love God both with the Good *and* the Evil Inclination.

This is indeed an encouragement. Our most potential self-offering is in the "redemption" of our negative or "shadow" aspects.

A Prayer
Make me, O Lord
  slow to anger
  slow to provoke
Make me, too
  quick to reconsider
  quick to praise
  quick to make peace
So may I be a true minister of reconciliation

Amen

August 16

A Thought

Stricken, saddened, sorrowing humanity needs words of healing. Fortunately there are words that can redeem the agony of doubt, words that can intellectually meet the most profound thinking that can be done: words that can minister to the most disturbed emotions: words that can bring peace where there is no peace: words of assurance and re-assurance: words of forgiveness and renewal, words of acceptance and achievement.

As Hosea said: "Take with you words."

A Prayer

O Word of God, incarnate
*   let Your words of hope inspire me*
*   let Your words of peace comfort me*
*   let Your words of life renew me*
*   let Your words of love bless me*
Through Him who is the Word

                        Amen

August 17

A Thought

By the "Divine Initiative", the offer of forgiveness comes and a right relationship to God is restored. God took that step in the Incarnation, Death and Resurrection of Christ. Forgiveness is dependent on nothing other than the acceptance of it. This is the heart of the Gospel.

A Prayer

May my love be expressed
*   in adoration towards You*
*   in sacrifice for others*
*   in acceptance of myself*
*   in service to the world*

                        Amen

August 18

A Thought

"Crisis", in Chinese, is composed of two ideograms. One represents "danger", the other "opportunity". This is indeed a symbolic reminder of the creative possibility of crisis. Crises are not usually pleasant, but, the nettle grasped, doors can open marvellously.

A Prayer

Look with Your searching eye at me, O God, and
  reveal to me my weaknesses
  clarify my uncertainties
So illumine my way, that the best I have to give
  may shine as a light in the world
Reflecting You, the Light of the world

Amen

August 19

A Thought

There is a corporate psychic "negativity" within the life
and soul of mankind that demands the redemptive activity of
God at both conscious and unconscious levels, as much as
the personal "shadow"—our negative side—does.
Forgiveness is the healing word where there is a healthy,
realistic and appropriate guilt. Every act of worship must
make real the "blotting out" and renewal that is life
redeeming. To the healthily guilty, "let us worship God" is a
declaration of assurance and peace.

A Prayer

Let me never wallow in my sin, Lord
  but only recognise that which separates me from Your love
  and offer it to You in faith
So may the blessing of relationship restored
  be the theme of all my praise

Amen

August 20

A Thought

"The followers of Christ are called by God," says Thomas
Merton (in *He is risen*), "not according to their
accomplishments, but according to His own purpose and

grace." This statement, Merton says, "effectively disposes of a Christian inferiority complex which makes people think that because they never have amounted to anything in the eyes of others, they can never amount to anything in the eyes of God."

A Prayer

May I spend this day, O God
  about Your business
    giving priority to the things of the
      Kingdom of Heaven
    finding perspective in the things
      of the kingdoms of this world
So may my balance be right
  and my day good
                              Amen

August 21

A Thought

It is the aim of "the Tempter" from the beginning to the end of life to destroy "the new creation" born of the presence of the Spirit. "He" never lets up. Christ found this out in His own life, for the "Satan" who left Jesus "for a season" returned many times . . . not least in Gethsemane and at Calvary. The process of growth in grace is the arena where the cosmic war between good and evil is focussed in the soul of each individual.

A Prayer

Let me not fear, O Lord
  the "powers of darkness in high places"
  for You are Lord of the universe
    Yours is the Power
Grant us the love that exorcises fear
Let Your love take over that love
  that it may be ever nearer "perfect"
                              Amen

August 22

A Thought

The healing of the soul, the self, is so much more than the restitution of the body. Indeed the acceptance that physical healing can not always be given may, in itself, be transformed into a ministry to the whole person. For those in the depths of pain, this is a hard saying: I say it however on the testimony of some who have suffered much.

A Prayer

Thanks be to You, O Lord
  for the witness of the good who suffer and know therefore
    Your presence
    Your redeeming grace
    Your transforming power
May their example be my inspiration

Amen

August 23

A Thought

What a subtle but profound thought is expressed by Jürgen Moltmann when he tells us that he had much to say at one time on "the resurrection of the crucified Jesus" but that now he wants to dwell much more on "the crucifixion of the risen Christ". It is the suffering of the eternal God in Christ that means so much.

A Prayer

Nothing in my hand I bring, O God
I simply cling to Your cross
Naked, I come to You for dress
Helpless, I look to You for grace
Nor will I be left unblessed
Thank You for Your Love

Amen

August 24

A Thought

In human relationships, sensitivity is a requirement for any who seek to offer healing. It is a word that speaks of subtle-ty, sureness and sympathy. It is a concept that puts importance on empathy and intuition. Sensitivity is built on respect for personality, so will never seek to invade privacy, but it also has a prophetic quality that enables the healing agent to sense need, despair or guilt in advance.

A Prayer

When all forsook Your Son and fled, O God
  Would I have been strong?
When they denied Your Son, O God
  could I have done otherwise?
When one betrayed Your Son, O Lord
  might it not have been me?
I thank You, God
  that You know what is in man
    and in me
And still forgive, accept and redeem

                    Amen

August 25

A Thought

"The road to this freedom (the liberty of the Spirit) as to every other experience is God's grace and leads to Golgotha". These words of Sister Eva of Friedenshort are true. The process is visible in the lives of the saints. But it is *so* hard to say it (because it is so easy to *say* it) to those who are undergoing exceptional suffering and cannot feel it to be true. Yet it is the constant testimony of those saintly folk who have suffered acutely over a long period, that it is the truth about life.

A Prayer

The day is past and over, Lord
  I have tried to give
    in loving care
      in compassion
        in prayer
May the gifts I have offered be to Your glory and for the good
  of those who have crossed my path
Now I am alone, abide with me
  For "without Thee, I cannot live"
May Your grace be sufficient for me
  Always

Amen

August 26

A Thought

Should worship be peaceful or disturbing? Should preaching be comforting or challenging? Elijah brought such a prophetic word that they called him the "troubler" of Israel. Jesus once said He came to bring, not peace, but a sword. So comfort or challenge? The answer must be "both". But the famous Scottish preacher, A. J. Gossip's demand that no sermon should be without comfort, tips the balance to that side.

A Prayer

When the circumstances of life separate me from those we would love most
  Bless me with the divine closeness
Help me accept courageously but graciously
  all that prevents commitment and self-giving
Then may I be enabled to offer my pent-up love
  in the service of mankind

Amen

August 27

A Thought

Jesus said: "Go ye into all the world". That is indeed a challenge! But He also used the "comfortable words: "Come unto me, all ye that labour and are heavy-laden, and I will give you rest".

The balance remains tipped to the side of comfort. We cannot really challenge the world while we are "weary and heavy-laden". So first, rest in the Lord, then truly say: "Here am I, send me".

A Prayer
When I feel the loneliness of life
  be a very present help, O Lord
When I feel the frustrations of life
  make me still, O Lord
When I become depressed about life
  lift up my eyes and heart, O Lord
When I lose control of life
  make me a captive, Lord
And so help me regain my true freedom

                    Amen

August 28

A Thought

There are many devotional classics but in any list these four will surely have a place: Augustine's *Confessions*, Thomas à Kempis' *Imitation of Christ*, John Bunyan's *Pilgrim's Progress* and Henry Drummond's *The Greatest Thing in the World*.

A Prayer
O Lord
  may I leave aside that which is grace-less
  may I love all that is grace-full

may I live graciously
And so, grace-filled
*   may I be an instrument of Your Peace*

Amen

August 29

A Thought

"All these things are against me"—as Jacob said over the loss of his sons. This is the story of life for some. Why does it happen to me? they say. Or does it happen to me partly at least because I am "me"? If the answer to the latter question is in the affirmative, it is time for us to ask questions about ourselves.

A Prayer

Give me, O Lord
*   unlimited patience*
*   unlimited understanding*
*   unlimited love*
Then I will be able to forgive
*   as I have been forgiven*
to bless
*   as I have been blessed*

Amen

August 30

A Thought

The Gospel is not a Gospel of dis-couragement, but of en-couragement, and no preacher dare forget that fact. Jesus came not to condemn the world, but to save it.

A Prayer

Teach me the discipline, Lord
   that is within
So may my inner strength be secured
   and my heart be at peace
Teach me the discipline, O Lord
   that comes from You
So may my life be lived
   within Your grasp of me

                   Amen

August 31

A Thought

It is a long time since John Baillie's *A Diary of Private Prayer* was published, but the prayers in it are, fundamentally, timeless. Like this, for example:

For the power Thou has given me
to lay hold of things unseen
For the strong sense I have that
this is not my home
For my restless heart, which nothing
finite can satisfy,
   I give Thee thanks, O God

A Prayer

Help me with pain, Lord
   the physical pain in my body
   the emotional pain in my heart
   the spiritual pain in my soul
   the pain of my mind
If, in my weakness, I must bear it
Make me to know Your strength is with me too

      Through Jesus Christ, our Lord   Amen

I triumph still!

September 1

A Thought

"Jesus came, the doors being shut". But is not that, miraculously now as it was then, exactly when we feel His presence?

A Prayer

Give me a sense of adventure, O Lord
  So that I may dream dreams and see visions
So work in me that I make them into realities
  that bring blessings
Grant me
  Deepened awareness
    so that I do not merely dream
Heightened intuition
    so that I am not limited by logic
  Acute perception
    so that I am able to calculate risks correctly

  Through Jesus Christ, our Lord   Amen

September 2

A Thought

Always, in times of pain, there is, somewhere, a rainbow.

A Prayer

Grant me O Lord the courage
  to climb the rainbow through the rain
  to feel the promise is not vain
  to know the eternal truth again –
    The Lord is risen!

    Amen

September 3

A Thought

"My will is not mine own
    till Thou has made it Thine;
If it would reach a monarch's throne
    it must its crown resign".

So George Matheson encapsulates the paradox that is, in human terms, foolishness, in divine terms, faith triumphant. The only way to growth is through death. The only way to resurrection is the way to the Cross. The only way to victory is through surrender.

And from the ground there blossoms red
Life that shall endless be.

A Prayer
It is not easy, willingly, O Lord
    to follow Your way
But I will, with grace abounding,
    give of myself to You
    trying to do Your will
    trying to give and not count the cost
    trying to be obedient at all times
When I fail, forgive
At all times, bless

                              Amen

September 4

A Thought

Spring will come. The great principle is true – both in nature and in the life of the Spirit. After death, there is new life. After the darkness there comes the dawn. After the Cross, and the descent into hell, there is, always, Resurrection.

A Prayer

When I pass through the valley of the shadows
  Keep my hope alive
      my faith real
      my peace intact
Then when the light at the end of the valley shows,
  Make me truly glad

                    Amen

September 5

A Thought

The desert, in the language of prayer is the place of both desolation and encounter with God. May times of desolation become times of encounter, because our "extremity" is indeed God's opportunity.

A Prayer

At dawn,
  grant me expectation
In the morning
  make me diligent
As the day goes on
  increase my serenity
Towards evening
  help me towards tranquillity
At the end of the day
  give me peace

                    Amen

September 6

A Thought

The drab and dreary vision of the Valley of Dry Bones in Ezekiel is not really about death. It is about resurrection, restoration and life. The Word, the Spirit and living in

relationship with God are all factors in that resurrection –
according to Ezekiel; or rather God through Ezekiel.

A Prayer
Give me life, O Lord
  through the healing of my body
            the healing of my memories
            the healing of my emotions
            the healing of my mind and
            the healing of my soul

Amen

September 7

A Thought

The Gospel record is full of the sensitivity of Christ.
"Sheep without a shepherd" sensed His attention even though
He had retired to quietness. Children and parents, rebuked by
the disciples, heard Him saying: "Suffer the little children to
come unto Me, and forbid them not". The key ... His
sensitivity to need, the knowledge He had of the human
condition, His ability to empathise with the sufferer, His
insight into the workings of the human heart. Sensitivity lies
at the very heart of God. He understands. He loves.

A Prayer
May I ever be a channel of blessing, Lord
  to the lonely
      to the distressed
          to the despairing
May I give of my hope
          my faith
            my love
  without thought of return

Amen

September 8

A Thought

Cardinal Suesens, the Roman Catholic writer, who played such a part in Vatican II writes profoundly on hope in his *Ways of the Spirit*

"Reflect upon winter in the woods. Trees which seem to be devoid of life are waiting for the sap to rise. Lopped branches enable others to take their place. Winter is not an end: it is a soil wherein the foliage of the future is nurtured. Winter is not desolation: it is a time of waiting. It is darkness before the dawn."

A Prayer
Looking unto Jesus, may I ever see
  Life
    Abundant
      Creative
        Eternal
And know that, through Him alone
  life is given to me

                    Amen

September 9

A Thought

It is hard to accept the pain of growth, for growing-pains are part of the evolving life of the Spirit. It is hard to reject "the flesh" in favour of "the spirit" and many a time in life great sorrow and bitter tears may wash our refusal to meet that demand. But the very confrontation we have had with reality, in all its stark sorrow or terrible tragedy may be *the ground of our becoming*, the soil in which new life is nurtured, the dismal death that leads to glorious resurrection.

A Prayer

I thank You, Lord
  that You did descend into hell
For You showed You save
  to the uttermost
That Your love reaches to the
  lowest depths of human darkness
May the memory of Your descent
  make my prayers the more ascend to You

                    Amen

September 10

A Thought

Consistency is an attribute of God as the Old Testament emphasises again and again. God does not change. God does not react on the basis of whim. He is the God of Abraham, Isaac and Jacob – and equally the God of David, John the Baptist, Paul and Christ.

For the Divine consistency expressed throughout the life of the Son of man who is Son of God, we ought to be eternally grateful.

"O Thou who changest not, abide with me".

A Prayer

Guard me
  Guide me
    Keep me
      Feed me
For I have no help but Yours, O God
But with that help, all things are possible to me

                    Amen

September 11

A Thought

Love has an ability to take adverse circumstances and see in them the opportunity for spiritual growth. It is indeed. To bear and to endure, in terms of Love, means taking, and accepting, grasping whatever is to our hurt and redeeming it so that it becomes a spiritually beneficial experience. *Nothing* need remain "negative" when the Spirit is present.

A Prayer
I bind unto myself, O God
  the strong name of the Trinity
    Rejoicing in Your Fatherhood
    Glorying in Jesus our Lord
    Growing in the Spirit
So may I know
  Three blessings in one

Amen

September 12

A Thought

There is a road that leads, so they say, from the very gates of heaven towards hell. Maybe. But, more important, there is a road that leads from the very gates of hell back towards heaven. Christ, who descended into hell, made sure of this for us.

A Prayer
May I draw on the resources that are within
And through courage, determination and will-power go on,
  O Lord
May I draw even more on the resources that are in You
I will then do all things through Christ, who strengtheneth me

Amen

September 13

A Thought

It is often a matter of agonising guilt if failure continues after a profound spiritual experience. It shouldn't happen again, we feel. But it does. And it will.

It may help to recall the timing of Christ's temptation crisis. It follows *immediately after* the declaration, at the descent of the Spirit, that He is God's "beloved Son" in whom He was well-pleased.

A Prayer
"When I survey the wondrous Cross"
  give me
    penitence
     assurance
      humility
And let me not put my trust
  in anything but the grace You give

              Amen

September 14

A Thought

God's demand to Elijah to forget about earthquakes, wind, fire and other natural circumstances as well as to put behind him his inner conflicts and suicidal inclinations, and simply listen to "the still, small voice" of Divine reality is a demand made to us all. It is a loving command made to us to *stop and listen!*

A Prayer
Watch with me, O God
  in temptation
    in pain
      in gloom

And by Your presence
  safeguard me
    comfort me
      uphold me

Amen

September 15

A Thought

The man or woman ready for God's service is the one who has seen and recognised the secret self and has come to creative terms with it.

It is no surprise that the truly human Jesus faced His own "other" ("shadow") side in the temptations, as subtle and powerful temptations as "Satan" could devise, for they concentrated on the possibility that Christ might, in His own interest, abuse His divine power.

That divine power which Jesus would not abuse became in fact the very power through which He could fulfil His mission.

The facing of our secret self can similarly become our strength.

A Prayer

Wherever I walk, O Lord
  may my light shine
    my love radiate
    my grace grow
    my peace bless
And so may others feel the presence of my Lord

Amen

September 16

A Thought

"It is more humanly beautiful to risk failure" writes Mark

Gibbard in his *Guide to Hidden Springs*, "searching for the hidden springs than to resign to the futurelessness of the wasteland. For the springs are there to be found."

A Prayer

Lead me, O Lord
  by still waters
And so
  restore my soul
Guide me, O Lord
  through Your still, small voice
And so
  renew my confidence
Walk with me, O Lord
  in the stillness and
    reassure me of Your nearness

                              Amen

September 17

A Thought

"God was in Christ, reconciling the world to Himself." Christ must be in us, compelling us to see that if our broken relationships are to be healed, we have no alternative but to take that first step towards reconciliation. The possibilities that will open up when that move is finally, even if reluctantly, made may well be the nearest things to miracles that we shall see in life.

A Prayer

The day You have given, O Lord
  is ending and
The darkness falls at Your behest
May our morning hymns have ascended
  to praise You
May You now sanctify our rest

                              Amen

September 18

A Thought

Spiritual exploration, like other forms of exploration, demands both risk and responsibility. Responsibility is needed otherwise we may be seduced and jump on any contemporary band-wagon; risk – because there is a call to "launch out into the deep" in Christianity.

"Abraham went out – not knowing whither he went." But look what followed!

Take risks – for the sake of Christ and His cause.

A Prayer

To risk myself, my future
  for You, O God
is to ask too much, too often

Yet without risk
  Your cause is stifled
  Without adventure
  Your work remains undone

Give me, O God, the grace
  to "take a chance" for You

                    Amen

September 19

A Thought

Do you know Christopher Logue's words?
  "Come to the edge" –
    It's too high
  "Come to the edge"
    We might fall
  "Come to the edge"
    And they did . . .
      And they flew!

A Prayer

May I, if You so call me
  be proud to be a fool for Christ's sake
May I undertake the humanly impossible
  in faith
May I accept the risks
  in trust
May I respond to the call to
  Divine adventure

                    Amen

September 20

A Thought

Responsibility is perhaps response-ability. It means making a response to a need, a situation, a challenge. The disciples showed response-ability. So did John Wilberforce, David Livingstone, George Fox, Martin Luther King, Alida Bosshardt, Mother Teresa and how many more? The dramatic irony of the situation is that having taken response-ability, they then showed 'creative irresponsibility', that is undertaking enterprises no 'responsible' person would and creating marvels by doing so!

A Prayer

What shall I render to You, O Lord
  for all Your benefits to me?
Give me a thankful heart
      a willing body
      a sharp and clear mind
      a dedicated soul

                    Amen

September 21

A Thought

The phrase "ministry of encouragement" is worth thought. The church must be a "community of encouragement" for after all Jesus came (He said) not to condemn, but to save. Why do we so often discourage people by criticism, by judgmental attitudes? Comfort, acceptance, support – against such concepts there is no law.

A Prayer

Make me a captive, Lord
  so may I find true freedom
Make me "poor in spirit" Lord
  so may I find true richness
Make me lowly of heart, Lord
  so may I feel true rest in my soul

                    Amen

September 22

A Thought

David, we are told, in a crisis "encouraged himself in the Lord, his God". Encouraged himself! There is a village in the north of England called "Pity Me". How often we make our home there! Self-pity is humanly understandable but is of no constructive help. We must fight and fight and fight again, said Hugh Gaitskell in a famous rallying call. So must we all, even when everything seems against us.

Encourage yourself!

A Prayer

Breathe on me, breath of God
  Fill me with life anew
That I may love what Thou dost love
  And do what Thou wouldst do

                    Amen

September 23

A Thought

How does one encourage oneself in the Lord our God? By recalling the things about God that are re-assuring. He is always the same – yesterday, today and for ever. He is utterly consistent. He makes things work together for good. He is infinite in forgiveness, loving-kindness and tender mercy. He is Love.

What encouragement!

A Prayer

Purge me and make me clean, O Lord
  Create a new heart within me
    And a right spirit

Spirit Divine, attend my birth into new life
  And make my body, heart, mind and soul together
    Your temple and Your home

                    Amen

September 24

A Thought

To see age in action is always encouraging – Emmanuel Shinwell addressing the Labour Party Conference in his nineties, Dr. Winifred Rushforth of Edinburgh developing Encounter Groups at 92, an organist – anonymous – enthusing over a new electronic instrument in his mid-eighties, having cycled to church! This is indeed a ministry of encouragement to us all!

A Prayer

May I so live that, in the daily race
  the things of God may hold the highest place

From that perspective, may I seek
  not glory
    or thanks
      or credit
But find my reward in the knowledge
  that I have tried to do Your will

                    Amen

September 25

A Thought

It is always a privilege to sense a saint of God in a
congregation, but there he was – mid-eighties, alert, singing
the songs of love with fervour and conviction; triumphant still
from the time when, in the trenches in the First World War,
he saw Christ beside him and heard His word of assurance,
just before he had to go "over the top" ("It all turned out just
as He said,"), to the present time of separation from his wife
through death. What a witness to the Faith!

A Prayer
Walk with me
  through the darkness, O Lord
Stay beside me through the shadows
Go ahead of me across the rocky way
Support me in the turbulent flood
So may I feel always in Your company

                    Amen

September 26

A Thought

The test of "the community of encouragement" – which
the church must be – is its ability to be supportive when the
situation is a difficult one. The ministry of encouragement is

not about bonhomie of a superficial kind. It is about the
ability to act supportively when things go seriously wrong. It
is about non-judgemental acceptance of situations that may
be threatening to its peace and welfare. It is about standing by
the member who has publicly failed and ensuring that, instead
of bringing him down and casting him out, he or she will be
held within the family and drawn upwards – encouraged – by
the community of grace.

A Prayer

Make me a force for good, O Lord
   so that, in the intense conflict between good and evil
   I may contribute to that which is of You
     and combat all that is foreign to Your will

                        Amen

September 27

A Thought

Life, Peter Ustinov has commented, is coming to realise all
the things you cannot do. The moral is that we must develop
any skill we have and, finding that we have the potential to do
something creative, go on and do it whatever happens. There
is no limit to our unused potential and no matter what our age
is, we must use all of it that we can.

A Prayer

Here we seek no abiding city
   we seek one to come
I press toward the mark
   for the prize of the high calling of God in Christ Jesus
Lord, nudge us ever forward, onward, outward, upward

                        Amen

September 28

A Thought

"The dreamers are the saviours of the world." So wrote James Allen in *As a Man Thinketh*. It sounds romantic and idealistic, but Allen is right. "The greatest achievements were at first and for a time dreams."

A Prayer

In my convictions
  make me firm
In my judgements
  make me sensitive
In my efforts to speak truth
  anchor me in love
And when I am criticised
  let me not be bitter
    but follow rather the example of Christ, my Lord

              Amen

September 29

A Thought

The sort of person Zacchaeus was – or had become – certainly assured him of power, but it deprived him of popularity. Detested for what he did and, in due course, for all he was, he became a lonely man, small in stature, but small in self-value too. Zacchaeus had neither inner strength nor friends to support him, so he was, naturally, interested in the man of whom he had heard so much good. He wanted to see "what Jesus looked like". It was the desire to look at Jesus that took him tree-climbing.

A Prayer

I praise You, O God
  from the heights of my joy
    and in the depths of my grief, sorrow and pain

I praise You, O God
  that You rejoice if I rejoice
    and weep when I weep
I thank You for the smile You bring to me
  and the tears You wipe away
I praise You O God
  I acknowledge You to be my Lord

                              Amen

September 30

A Thought

There are walls and barriers that men create to try to stifle contact and conversation, but they only succeed in part. Dietrich Bonhoeffer was put to death, but he still speaks to the world. Christ was crucified in an effort to stop His message and His influence. But near 2,000 years later, it is still proclaimed.

Yes, indeed, whatever men do, "the Lord reigneth".

A Prayer
Make me an agent of reconciliation
  so that
      where division reigns
      where communication ceases
    where love has gone
  I draw people together
    with cords of love
So may they be bound together
  through Him to whom I am bound
Even Jesus Christ, our Lord

                              Amen

The Spirit and the Silence

October 1

A Thought

"The Healing of the Memories" is a phrase of great beauty and profundity. I see it as a process involving the activity of the Spirit, not only within our conscious understanding, but deep in the hidden places psychology calls the "unconscious". It has to do with realisation, acceptance, forgiveness and transformation. In other words with "integration through the Spirit".

A Prayer
In times of pressure
  grant me peace
In times of harassment
  grant me hope
In times of stress
  grant me serenity
In times of sadness
  grant me strength
At all times offer me
  Your benediction

> *Through Jesus Christ, our Lord   Amen*

October 2

A Thought

Cardinal Suesens, the famous Roman Catholic writer, said at Pentecost, 1974: "I believe in the surprises of the Holy Spirit."

There are indeed many of them, if we have the eyes of faith.

A Prayer
Grant me
  the sense of wonder that says:
    "Speak Lord, I hear"
  the sense of repentance that pleads:

"Wash me ... and I shall be clean"
the sense of gladness that shouts:
"He makes all things new"
Thus may I be truly a new creation

Amen

October 3

A Thought

Metropolitan Ignatias offered these words on the Holy Spirit at a World Council of Churches meeting in 1968.
"Without the Holy Spirit
God is far away
Christ stays in the past
the Gospel is simply an organisation
authority a matter of propaganda
the liturgy is no more than an evolution
Christian loving, a slave morality"

A Prayer
Touch me
  with Your Spirit
Embrace me
  in Your Love
Enfold me
  in Your Peace
Uphold me
  in Your Strength

Amen

October 4

A Thought

Metropolitan Ignatias goes on:
"But in the Holy Spirit
the cosmos is resurrected and grows
with the birth pangs of the Kingdom

the Risen Christ is there
the Gospel is the power of life
the Church shows forth the life of the Trinity
authority is a liberating service
mission is a Pentecost
the liturgy is both renewal and anticipation
human action is deified."

A Prayer

"Come, holy Dove
  expand Thy wings
  the wings of peaceful love"
Make me conscious of
  the protection of the Spirit
  the cleansing of the Spirit
  renewal by the Spirit
Breathe on me, breath of God
Fill me with life anew

Amen

October 5

A Thought

Who . . . or what . . . would control the life of Christ?
That was the battle He fought in the desert.
To whom would Paul belong and whom must he serve?
These were the issues he faced in the desert of Arabia.
How shall we find the way to integration and wholeness?
That is the question we take to the stillness of our desert,
wherever it may be.
The answer we shall discover, as Paul did, in partnership
with the Spirit.

A Prayer

Make me a medium of Your peace
  to the anxious, frightened, frustrated, lonely and distressed

May the peace "which passes understanding" be found
  in the caring I convey and
  in the serenity I share

                    Amen

October 6

A Thought

Dependence on the Holy Spirit is sometimes made an excuse for doing no homework before speaking, but the Holy Spirit cannot, of course, work on nothing. It is the well-stored, disciplined mind that is the vehicle of the Spirit.

A Prayer
Grant me the word of grace
  to troubled souls
Let me show the act of grace
  to unhappy lives
Make me living grace
  to all with whom I have to do

                    Amen

October 7

A Thought

There is a ministry of silence in the Christian faith. One element in it is the need for silence about others. St. Paul said on sensationalism and gossip: "Love is not glad when things go wrong; love rejoices in the truth". If we cannot speak well of people, perhaps we are called to keep silence about them.

A Prayer
Let me no more my comfort draw
  From my frail hold of Thee
In this alone rejoice with awe
  Thy mighty grasp of me
So may I feel the everlasting arms beneath me

                    Amen

October 8

A Thought

There is a place for silence in prayer. It is the time when the asking stops and the listening begins: a time when there is a genuine "waiting on the Lord" and a receptiveness to His presence. That is the time when the Spirit comes.

A Prayer
In the silence
   I adore
In the silence
   I repent
In the silence
   I give thanks
In the silence
   I pray
But in the silence, too
   I listen
"Speak, Lord, for Thy servant heareth"

                            Amen

October 9

A Thought

So much of prayer is words addressed to God – and properly so. We must voice our praises, our thanks, our confessions, our dedication. But in any relationship there must be conversation, not monologue. In other words in our relationship with God, He too must speak, and we must – in silence – listen.

A Prayer
Give me an understanding of what I do to others
   an appreciation of what others do for me

Give me respect for another's personality and freedom
  So that I do not force on them
    my care-full anxiety or
    my care-less words
May I then offer more, not less
  but always at the right time

Amen

October 10

A Thought

A striking element in the ministry of silence is the silence of
dignity, that silence displayed by our Lord when blasphemous
questions were thrown at Him by His accusers. "He
answered them nothing."

There are times when the only answer to the things people
say is dignified silence.

A Prayer

May I live each day with respect
  For all that is good in the past
  With understanding of all that is part of the present
  With enthusiasm for all that is now in the future
In the company of Him who is the same yesterday, today
  and for ever

Amen

October 11

A Thought

A silence that must be recovered is the silence of awe and
wonder, the reaction so often displayed in biblical times in the
presence of God. Respect is not a contemporary
characteristic – whether it be for property, old age,
relationships of intimacy or even God.

The recovery of the silence of awe before the One who is
holy and who has shown His love in Christ, is a priority. It
must begin within the church itself.

A Prayer

For the unity we have
  We thank You, O God
For the unity not yet possible
  We ask the power to search
Restore the shattered Cross
  through the Power of Your Spirit
And gather, in Your own good time
  all Christians in true communion

                              Amen

October 12

A Thought

More is often said by silence than by sounds. Think of that moment of silent wonder in the presence of holy beauty ... Think of the effect of a period of silence in worship, music or meditation ... Think how much more is said by silent loving embrace in bereavement than halting, hesitant words, however sincere, can say ... Think of the silences of love ...

"Be still ..."

A Prayer

Help me to look at everything around me, O God
  and find reason for Praise
Help me to listen to the sounds of nature, O God
  and find reason to give Thanks
Help me notice the signs of need, O God
  and be ready to respond
Help me to feel the pain of all, O God
  and be there to help with love

                              Amen

October 13

A Thought

Hold to the silence of wonder! It is the *awe-full* silence that human beings should feel in the presence of the holy; the silence the numinous compels: the silence of speechlessness that recognition of the divine dimension demands.

It is a silence our over-sophisticated society and perhaps even our churches need to know.

A Prayer

Make me like salt, O Lord
  so that, retaining "the savour" through grace
    I may feed society with love
    I may stimulate society to life
    I may encourage society by example

                              Amen

October 14

A Thought

It is essentially human to retaliate when accusations are made against us. It may even be right to do so on occasions. But there is, in Christ's example *(see October 10),* a reminder of the power of the silence of conviction, the silence of assurance that comes from a heart that remains unaffected and untouched by trivial taunts and heartless hate. This is the silence of dignity shown by Jesus when, in response to His accusers, He answered nothing.

A Prayer

May the holiness I seek, O Lord
  be the holiness I find in You
May the grace I convey, O Lord
  be the grace that is from You
May the hope I offer, O Lord
  be the hope that is in You
May the life that I live, O Lord
  be the life You live in me

                              Amen

October 15

A Thought

Wendy Robinson (in *Exploring Silence*) talks of four "shapes of silence" – The Silence of Availability (necessary passivity); The Silence of Growth (the silence of gestation); Silence beyond Words (pure silence – after words, the silence of lovers) and The Silence of the Pieta (the silence of suffering and the mystery of death). These are indeed silences to be explored – with Wendy (see Book References).

A Prayer
How wonderful, O God
  is the Divine humility
You washed feet
  You had no place to lay Your head
    You became obedient unto death
      despising its shame
Let Your humility invade me
  so that I be no more
    proud and arrogant
      self-laudatory and loud
but reflect Your humility

Amen

October 16

A Thought

The Christian community will bless the world if it can do anything to contribute to the restoration of silence as a therapeutic component in the healing of mankind.

A Prayer
Give me the ability to be still
  so that my stillness will help others
Give me the quality of peace
  so that my inner calm will calm others

Give me the attitude of compassion
  so that I am found to be caring
Give me the characteristics of Christ
  so that I may bring blessings in His name

Amen

October 17

A Thought

"There is such a thin line between tears and laughter" a letter-writer says. And between love and hate. And between anger and reconciliation. The presence of the Spirit is so necessary when we balance on these lines – to nudge us to the right side.

A Prayer
When we walk through
  a vale of tears
    take our hands, O Lord
When we dance over
  a mountain of laughter
    clap Your hands, O Lord
When we stand in the
  valley of decision
    take our arm, O Lord
And let us know that, always
  those everlasting arms are underneath

Amen

October 18

A Thought

Too often we expect miracles from heaven and forget the need to "prepare the way of the Lord". To plan for the Spirit is not to deny His power, but to acknowledge it.

A Prayer

I wait on You, O God
  in reverence
    in humility
      in penitence
        in trust
May the finitude of my expectation
  be swamped in the infinity of Your grace
So waiting, may I be filled

Amen

October 19

A Thought

Grace is a gift and grace brings growth. It is a gift nothing we can do can earn. It brings growth for it is the energy of the Spirit promised by Christ. Grace is therefore "sufficient" for us.

There is no higher gift than "grace".

A Prayer

Pour out Your Spirit on me
  O Lord
May I learn the vibrations
  of that Spirit
May I feel the energy
  of that Spirit
So that I may pour out on others
  the gift that has been given to me

Amen

October 20

A Thought

In every part of life, one principle holds true. We cannot "give out" if we do not "take in".

Without the falling rain, the reservoirs diminish. Without the gentle breeze the windmill stays motionless. Without the gift of water from the sky, the rivers fail and the mountain streams dry up. Without taking in breath, there is no hope in life. Without the appropriate amount of food, strength goes. Without sleep, we have no energy.

It is the same in the life of the Spirit.

A Prayer
Grant me, O God
   the generosity to give
      without counting the cost to me
   the grace to receive
      without counting the cost to others
Then shall I know the joy both of giving and receiving
   gratefully
      graciously

                              Amen

October 21

A Thought

"I will lift up mine eyes to the hills. From whence cometh my help? My help cometh from the Lord."

While saints have been found in the city, they have tended to nourish their souls on the hills or in the desert; near the earth; often in solitude. Jesus was crucified in or around the city. The strength He needed to face it, He found on the hillside, or in a garden.

A Prayer
May the "still dews of quietness"
   drop around me and on me
So stilled, may I radiate peace
   everywhere
And widen the area of serenity

                              Amen

October 22

A Thought

I paraphrase some very important words of Paul in
Philippians 4:11–12. "In every situation I have been in," says
Paul (and he gives a list of very traumatic situations) "I have
found a creative opportunity. I have, within the limits of any
given set of circumstances however intolerable, found a way
to use those circumstances positively. And so, while accepting
these limitations as reality – as 'the things that cannot be
changed' – I have found in and through them true
contentment."

Limitation, hostility and adversity are, spiritually speaking,
learning situations. They develop our resources, so increasing
our faith and evolving our maturity. As the *New English
Bible* puts it: "I have learned to find resources in myself
whatever the circumstances".

A Prayer

O God grant me
  strength of body
    so that I may be creative for Your Kingdom
  strength of mind
    so that I may think clearly about Your Kingdom
  strength of will
    so that I may discipline myself for the Kingdom
  strength of faith
    so that I may believe in the things of the Kingdom

Amen

October 23

A Thought

"Try the spirits," we are told, "to see if they are of God."
Here is the test. Good spirits console and fortify. Evil spirits
afflict, agitate and depress.

A Prayer

The Lord bless you and keep you
The Lord make His face to shine upon you
and be gracious unto you
The Lord lift up His countenance upon you
and give you peace

Amen

October 24

A Thought

The Holy Spirit produces, not disorder but order. That is an important guideline in making any assessment of manifestations claimed to be of "the Spirit".

A Prayer

Grant, O Lord that
Forgetting the things which are behind
I may reach forward energetically
Remembering the things which are behind
I may the more "press toward the mark"
for the prize of the high calling of God in Christ Jesus
So may I learn of Your purpose
and follow Your path

Amen

October 25

A Thought

St. Ignatius Loyola, we are told, found that daydreams of his own glory, while pleasant at the time, left him tired, bored and sad, while his dreams of being a second St. Francis left him content and joyful. Thus he found he was sifting his emotions and beginning to see clearly which were the promptings of the Spirit. This he later called "Discernment of Spirits".

A Prayer

Make me aware, O God
*   when it is Your voice I hear*
Then will I do Your will
*   and follow Your Way*

Help me always
*   to test the spirits*
*   to see what is of God and*
*   to follow these*

Amen

October 26

A Thought

The late John Baillie who wrote (among other things) *Invitation to Pilgrimage* and *A Diary of Private Prayer*, tells us there never was a time when he was not aware of God. He was brought up "within" the faith.

Sometimes we put great stress – and not without reason – on a dramatic conversion, but steady growth in grace, ending in public commitment, is genuine, too.

A Prayer

May I, O Lord, be
*   sure and steadfast*
My anchor dropped deeply
*   in Your love*
So may I reach the desired haven

Amen

October 27

A Thought

Mother Mary Clare has a word for us in times when prayer is difficult. She says: "Prayer is not conditioned by clock-time. It is a total relationship with God that enables us to move easily from the day to day demands of life into a loving familiarity with God."

A Prayer
Help me to find
   time to encourage
   time to forgive
   time to be still
   time to rise up
Let me never allow my time
   to be so full that I cannot serve

                    Amen

October 28

A Thought

The search for Truth is like climbing a mountain. We all start from different bases. We cannot see each other, so we do not know who is on the way or where. Truth is found only when we reach the top for there everything is in perspective.

We are all climbers, moving towards truth, but we come to it from different directions.

The main thing is to Keep Climbing!

A Prayer
I ask not to see
I ask not to know
   I ask only to be used

                    (A prayer of Cardinal Newman)

October 29

A Thought

"What is that to thee? Follow thou me!"

These sharp words to Peter at the end of St. John's Gospel constitute the call to obedience Jesus issued regularly. The call involves total commitment, leaving other people's affairs out of our reckoning, and being nonconformist if necessary.

It is not easy to be "different". It may nevertheless be a demand we have to meet in Christian discipleship, helped by the Spirit.

A Prayer

O God, make it my concern
  to seek first Your Kingdom and its righteousness
  leaving other things to look after themselves

  to love You with heart and soul
  and mind and strength
  and my neighbour as myself

  to bear all things
  believe all things
  hope all things

So may my balance be right
  and my perspective clear

Amen

October 30

A Thought

If you are worried because you feel you have committed the so-called "sin against the Holy Spirit", then you need worry no more. The point about that sin is that you simply do not have the capacity to worry about it. So hardened is the heart that a state is reached where there is total inability to distinguish evil from good. Those who called Jesus "Beelzebub" had nearly reached that most dangerous spiritual condition. When you do not see any difference between Jesus and Satan, then it is time to worry about being almost beyond forgiveness. For forgiveness is a response to repentance. If the capacity for repentance has gone, how can forgiveness come?

A Prayer

Forgive, O Lord, my foolish ways
  my lustful heart
  my ill-tempered attitude
  my envy
  my disregard of others
And change these foolish ways
  to better things

                    Amen

October 31

A Thought

There are times when we *are* called to nonconformity!
Faith triumphant may even involve being "a fool for Christ's
sake".

Thoreau wrote: "If a man does not keep pace with his
companions, perhaps it is because he hears a different
drummer. Let him step to the music he hears, however
measured and far away . . ."

A Prayer

Give me the strength
                courage
                    faith
   to be different
     separated
       a fool for Christ's sake
If this be Your will
May I then stand and withstand
   for Your sake

Through Jesus Christ, our Lord   Amen

Healing Power

November 1

A Thought

The search for "the healing of the memories" ends at the table of the Lord, for there the source of grace and the experience of grace is made real.

The Sacrament is not merely a memorial. It is a *means* of grace. *There* is the memory that heals. "This do in remembrance of me." "You must continue to do this to make you remember me" (William Barclay).

A Prayer

You came, O Lord,
  sweet influence to impart

I thank You for the influence
  that surrounded me through others' faith
  the influence that comes through Word and Sacrament
  the influence I feel through the community of grace

I thank You for the inflow of the Spirit

Through Jesus Christ, our Lord   Amen

November 2

A Thought

Compassion is an outgoing caring that has no power aspect to it. It is the radiation of loving concern for another, because the love of Christ "constraineth us".

A Prayer

Lord grant me the power to see ourselves as others see us
And so to learn from my effect on others
  that I reflect You

Amen

November 3

A Thought

The phone rang in the middle of the night. It was a friend of a friend who wanted to commit suicide.

"I should never have been born," she said, "I didn't want to be born and no-one wanted me to be born".

I felt I had to go to her, to show her she was wanted *now*. So I went.

I think it helped. At least she is − years later − alive and happy.

A Prayer

Make me a channel of your peace
　Where there is despair, let me bring hope
　Where there is sadness, let me bring joy
　Where there is hatred, let me bring love

　　　　　　　　Amen
　　　　　(based on words by Sebastian Temple)

November 4

A Thought

Colonel Alida Bosshardt, who worked in the Red Light area of Amsterdam for 27 years, speaks of the broken contact between God and man and the need for reconciliation. So evangelism involves the ministry of the Word, the offering of the Gospel to all wherever they are and however far off the awful country to which they have gone, "with the purpose of brining them to the faith".

A Prayer
Here am I, Lord
  send me
    with words of comfort
      gestures of love
        thoughts of strength
          hearts of hope
  to all Your people

Amen

November 5

A Thought

Alida Bosshardt's view of pastoral care is that it is "the work of the Shepherd bringing comfort and guidance through the Word in order to build up faith and deepen spiritual lives". The purpose of both evangelism and pastoral care is "the preaching of the Word that is not of ourselves but is of God; the Word of forgiveness, renewal and hope, revealed in and through Christ". It is "Christ for the world, the world for Christ".

A Prayer
Turning my eyes upon You, O God
  and looking on the face of Christ
May I find the cares of the world
  pass into oblivion

Amen

November 6

A Thought

Suffering was something Christ knew, because it was part of being human in the free world God had made. Illness is something that should not be. If there is dis-ease present within us, something has gone wrong that need not have done so.

It is God's will that we do all we can to relieve dis-ease.

A Prayer
In days of uncertainty
  be sure and steadfast, O Lord
In days of unknowing
  touch the deadened intuition
  heal shattered faith
In days of rejection
  renew Your acceptance of us, as we are
In days of resurrection
  give us joy and peace

                    Amen

November 7

A Thought

Healing ministry is not an extra-ordinary ministry within the church, but *normal* ministry. Jesus used two phrases, not one, in His commands to His disciples. They were "Preach the Gospel" *and* "Heal the sick". Both are mandatory.

A Prayer
Grant me insight, O Lord
  into myself
  into others and
  into the ways of the Spirit
Then may I find the doorway
  to growth in grace
  and the likeness of Jesus Christ

                    Amen

November 8

A Thought

The more I think about the relationship between the physical, the mental, the emotional and the spiritual, the more fascinating becomes the concept of health, and the more important our constant consideration of the nature of healing. Dis-ease in any part does seem related to dis-ease of the whole.

A Prayer
Graciously deal with me O God
  when I fall short of Your hopes
  when I compromise Your standards
  when I disobey Your will
  when I fail in charity
Through your grace, may I begin again
  and feel hope-full

Amen

November 9

A Thought

Martin Israel has a profound understanding of the inner healing processes and of the healing of the memories. Accepting as he does, "the corruption that lies deeply within us", he writes in *Smouldering Fire*: "The work of the Spirit in regenerating the unconscious mind by redeeming deeply hidden paradoxes is the basis of the healing process". Integration is, I say again, through the Spirit.

A Prayer
The good that I would,
  I do not, O Lord
The evil that I would not,
  That I do

Who shall deliver me from this death,
  the law in my members that when
  I would do good, evil is present within me?
I thank God
  "Through Jesus Christ, our Lord"

                    Amen

November 10

A Thought

So many of our assessments of people are based either on limited knowledge or lack of real knowledge that it is not surprising that we often err in our judgements. We cannot know everything about everyone, but at least the realisation of that limitation will make us cautious in the evaluations to which we commit ourselves.

A Prayer
Make me care-full in judgement
  truth-full in criticism
  grace-full in relationship
  wonder-full in encounter
Never let me lose the sense of the holy
  in You and Your creation

                    Amen

November 11

A Thought

The fifth of six steps suggested for those who "seek to love creatively" is this: "Whatever your profession or occupation, cultivate the listening ear, the penetrating mind, the observant eye, the loving heart, the gentle voice and the humble spirit."

A Prayer

O God,

strengthen within me the will to serve
create within me the heart to love
renew within me the desire to give
seal within me the gifts of grace

Amen

November 12

A Thought

"I saw you coming down the western road,
My heart laid down its load"
That Chinese couplet of the fourth century BC sums up the
wonder of the loving heart.

A Prayer

Let peace begin with me, O Lord
For only so, can I be a peace-maker
Let truth begin with me, O Lord
For only so, can I forward truth in the world
Let Love begin with me, O Lord
For only so, can I add to the love
the world needs

Amen

November 13

A Thought

The concept of the Logos is used by John in his Gospel to
proclaim two of the great purposes of the Word, who is
Christ. The first is that He is *the Revealer of God* and th
second that He is *the Saviour of Men*. In both capacities, H
is God's *healing* Word.

A Prayer
Draw me nearer
    nearer
        nearer, O Lord
So that I receive from You
    grace
        power
            peace
Making me a more effective disciple

                    Amen

November 14

A Thought

The human perspective and the divine perspective are so different. What seems to be a serious sin in the understanding of men – and this often depends largely on the mores of the moment or the current cultural context – may look very different to the One who sees not in part, but in whole, not through a glass darkly, but with the clarity and charity of the divine understanding.

It is this attribute of God that makes so truly for healing. We may hide our faults and failings from our friends and fear the disillusionment that surely must follow their discovery, but God is a different proposition. He is (as St. John reminds us, 2:25) "well aware of what human nature is like". He knows *before* we ask, confess or plead. It is out of His understanding of us in our totality that healing begins.

A Prayer
Glow, with Your "Fire Divine", O God
    in my heart
make it radiant
    warm
        loving

enfolding others in its "warm embrace"
  as You have enfolded us
    in the embrace of Your love

Amen

November 15

A Thought

God sees our worst before others – or even we ourselves – do. Is that a counsel of despair? It is the reverse. It is the word of hope we need, the word of comfort for which we yearn. Healing begins, is continued and ends in the divine awareness, understanding, forgiveness, acceptance and sanctification of us. It is there life begins anew.

A Prayer

Begin Your miracle of grace in me, O Lord
  through Jesus Christ
Continue the growth of grace in me, O Lord
  through Jesus Christ
Finish Your new creation of me, O Lord
  through Jesus Christ
And I will bless You, the author and finisher of my faith

Amen

November 16

A Thought

In the pastoral care of people, it is no use pretending they are where they ought to be or that they are what they are meant to be, when the reality is quite different. The only hope for ministry begins with the acceptance that they are what they are, "warts and all". Then, and only then, will the road to achievement open up.

A Prayer
Accept me, Lord
  Just as I am
     confused
     compromising
     capricious
Make me, Lord
  what You want me to be

And this I leave in Your hands

                    Amen

November 17

A Thought

The minister, showing us his Weimar church, said a lot about its architecture, its stained glass, its organ. He did not say his wife was dying.

"The show must go on" is a great tradition that is not confined to the stage. There is often much personal suffering, unseen, behind pastoral ministry.

A Prayer
Let my face be bright
  though my heart be heavy
Let my love be real
  though love has been lost
Let my care be rich
  though care I have not
Let me give of friendship
  even when I stand alone
The grace to do this I ask
  through Jesus Christ, our Lord

                    Amen

November 18

A Thought

The Paraclete is the healer in three ways: first, the Spirit is
the Comforter in the root meaning of that word. The Spirit
gives strength. The Spirit is, secondly, the *Consoler* for we
need consolation. Thirdly, the Spirit of our *Advocate.* He
speaks on our behalf.

"The Spirit itself makes the intercession for us." That is
good news, for that is a healing process indeed.

A Prayer

I rejoice in the Good News
  God is Love!
  Christ is risen!
  The Spirit has come!
  Forgiveness is free!
I bless You for this News
  for it leads to life

                    Amen

November 19

A Thought

"Deep speaks to deep" says the Psalmist. It *is* true —
psychologically and spiritually. So beware if you listen to or
hear part of such a conversation, for you may be on another
level and you may misunderstand.

A Prayer

Give me integrity, O Lord
  and let me not then worry about criticism
Give me conviction, O Lord
  and help me triumph over hurt
Give me peace, O Lord,
  so shall I be unmoved by hostility

                    Amen

November 20

A Thought

It is God's will that (as Paul says in I Timothy 2:4) "all men shall be saved and come to a knowledge of the truth". In the end, all will return to the God who made them if they can, like the Prodigal Son, "come to themselves".

So God waits in patience for His recalcitrant people, not in anger or irritation, but with the Divine longing that lies eternally in His heart.

We are called to reflect that patience.

A Prayer

O God, I love You
  not because "I hope for heaven thereby"
  but because You first loved me
  Seal that relationship
    through grace and faith
Then may I live in relationship to You
  all the days of my life

                    Amen

November 21

A Thought

Of all the Old Testament passages dealing with "pastoral" work, that which comes from Ezekiel (34:11, 15–16, NEB), is surely the most moving: "I myself will tend my flock, I myself pen them in their fold, says the Lord God . . . . I will search for the lost, recover the straggler, bandage the hurt, strengthen the sick, leave the healthy and strong to play, and give them their proper food."

A Prayer

Faced by the grief and pain of mankind,
  Grant me Your understanding, O Lord
    so that I may help constructively

minister creatively
encourage graciously
So may my ministry be seen as guided and upheld by You

Amen

November 22

A Thought

The Master helps and heals today through the power of the Holy Spirit He promised. If this is not reality, then the Gospel is a mockery. It is reality and so the ministry "in His name" must go on to demonstrate not only His power in the past but the promise of the "greater works" that will bear witness to His power today. "His touch has not lost its ancient power".

A Prayer

Grant me Your peace, O God
as I look back over this day
and repent of its wrongs
as I sleep this night
as I face tomorrow
and all it brings for me to do
Let me wake refreshed and ready
to serve You more and more

Amen

November 23

A Thought

Sensitivity is not sentimentality. It is an attitude that sometimes has to express itself in strength. It was the sensitivity of Christ to the need to recognise the human freedom and responsibility that allowed the rich young ruler to leave whereas sentimentality or sympathy of a softer kind might have wanted to try to ease his way into the Kingdom. Love had the sensitivity to let the young man go.

A Prayer
I triumph still
  If You abide with me
So let Your presence be with me
  Always

                    Amen

November 24

A Thought

"To gain insight into oneself, to come to oneself, to learn to know oneself" says Alida Bosshardt, "all this happens when Christianity functions properly. Efficient social work functions similarly. Christianity has an extra dimension however. There is a greater Power at work. It is a Power that can totally change a person and lead to conversion."

A Prayer
Touch my heart Lord, and let there be
  compassion
    tenderness
      gentleness
        love
  in what I offer to those in need

                    Amen

November 25

A Thought

Joy, an inner quality, rather than an outward emotional or physical expression, is an attribute of God Himself, so human joy is a reflection of Divine joy just as love is a reflection of the Divine love.

"Rejoice always,
Again, I say, rejoice"

A Prayer

May I in heavenly love abide
  and feel secure
May I in heavenly joy abide
  and feel glad
May I in heavenly grace abide
  and feel at peace

Amen

November 26

A Thought

Christian joy is not an ethereal quality associated only with
the soul, nor is it merely pleasurable gratification associated
with the body. It is a product of grace and faith that is related
to our wholeness, and this can be felt only when two
yearnings are satisfied – our deeply felt spiritual needs and
our legitimate delight in the senses, when dedicated to the
glory of God.

A Prayer

I see You, O God
  in the beauty of nature
I sense You, O God
  in the mystery of revelation
I feel You, O God
  in the "love I receive"
I offer You, O God
  the love I can give

Amen

November 27

A Thought

One of the most healing words in the Bible is the word
"redemption". It whispers of sin forgiven. It speaks of new
opportunity. It sings of freedom and it shouts of hope.

A Prayer

Let me not proclaim my failings, Lord
  You know them all
    and whisper forgiveness
Let me rather proclaim Your love, O Lord
  I know it for
    I have felt it often
May the value of my failings be
  the door they open
    to help others towards forgiveness, too

Amen

November 28

A Thought

"Redemption . . . sings of freedom" – the freedom implicit in the changed new life. It deals not only with the past through the renewal of the present. It looks to the future. It opens inner doors, releases creativity, offers true liberty. It must therefore shout "hope"!

A Prayer

I am saved by hope, O Lord
  The sense of Your constancy
  The knowledge of Your final victory
  The assurance of Your continuing presence
    lighten and gladden my future
May I walk in Your light
  and rejoice in Your love

Amen

November 29

A Thought

Redemption is concerned with the healing of the memories, both conscious and unconscious – beyond our conscious awareness. It is only as the Holy Spirit first probes, then penetrates the unconscious areas of our lives that "conversion", or fundamental change occurs.

It is in these deepest, inner areas that the Holy Spirit must move in redemptive activity and renewing grace.

A Prayer

Remember me, O Lord
* in my weaknesses but also*
*   in my strengths*
* in my failings but also*
*   in my successes*
Grant me the honesty to see
* where I have been wrong*
And the humility to acknowledge
* where I have had success*
And through both
* lead me toward true righteousness*

Amen

November 30

A Thought

The miracle of redemption is that the worst we have or are becomes the most potentially creative part of ourselves that we can offer. Selfish aggressiveness redeemed can become dedicated energy devoted to the blessing of mankind. Lust redeemed can be the compassion of love and the love of compassion that ministers to need. Anxiety understood can become a quality of peace-fulness that "passes understanding" and passes its tranquillity to others.

Redemption is the activity of God in Christ through the Spirit and only in that context is it a wholly healing process.

A Prayer

May my whole being reflect
  the grace of our Lord Jesus Christ
  the love of God and
  the fellowship of the Holy Spirit, the Comforter

Through Jesus Christ, our Lord   Amen

God with us

December 1

A Thought

When Dr. John White one of the most famous ministers ever at the Barony Church in Glasgow, was asked the secret of his spiritual resources, he answered simply: "I met a Man".

Grace is mediated in many ways – a distant encounter with a voice, a close encounter of a fleeting kind with someone on the path, a loving relationship with a like mind or heart, an intimate and a profound meeting of souls across a decade, the life-long companionship of another. There is someone somewhere who has blessed your way.

I met a man . . .
I met a woman . . .
I met . . .

A Prayer

Thank You, O God
  for those with whom I have found rapport
  for those in whom I have sensed Your presence
  for those through whom I have gained in insight
  for those whom I have loved and who have loved me

Thanks be to You, O God, for meetings
  with those who do us good

Through Jesus Christ, our Lord   Amen

December 2

A Thought

"Take with you words," said Hosea *(see August 16)*. Words can be an instrument of peace, an orchestration of joy, a symphony of the sounds of salvation.

Through words, Christ the Word is made known.

A Prayer
I wait on You, O God
  to renew my strength
    to run and not be weary
      to walk and not faint
May I be renewed in my waiting

Amen

December 3

A Thought

To enter the human condition on the stage of history, at the time He did and in the place He did, was to face the problems of expectation. For Israel was earnestly looking for the Messiah who would deliver the Rome-dominated nation from its oppressors, the One who would "redeem Israel".

Jesus was crucified because He did not come up to expectations.

A Prayer
May the spirit of reconciliation
  be in me, O God
So that I may reconcile and bless wherever I go
So may I truly be
  a minister of reconciliation

Amen

December 4

A Thought

When I met that great Japanese Christian, Toyohiko Kagawa, *The Saint in the Slums*, the concept of humility, as I had always envisaged it, became incarnate. His influence (as my recording it some 20 or more years later shows) has remained. I met a man of grace, graciousness and gracefulness.

True humility is, in truth, a mark of the man in Christ.

A Prayer

As I journey on, dear Lord
  be a companion on my way
  be a courier for my way
  be a welcoming host at the end of the way
So may I feel I have never been alone on the journey

Amen

December 5

A Thought

Humility is a mark of the Christian. It will always "increase" us rather than decrease us, if we can find the secret of it. It is when we set out to be boastful and conceited that we lose spiritual stature for Love "vaunteth not itself, is not puffed up". It is only when we clothe ourselves in the garments of humility that we truly grow.

A Prayer

Give me tolerance, O Lord
  so that I
    bear with the unbearable
    have patience with the trying
    have understanding for the provoking
And when I come near to my wits' end
  Grant me yet more grace

Amen

December 6

A Thought

Humility is not a denial of one's worth. It is a recognition of it.

A Prayer

Grant me, O God
  the grace of humility

In all my labours
  prevent me from concern with prestige, position and
  popularity
Make my satisfaction and my pleasure
  the doing of Your will

Amen

December 7

A Thought

We are, Paul tells us, "letters from Christ" (II Corinthians 3:3). We have therefore a pastoral purpose to fulfil on paper *and* in person.

A Prayer

Help me to feel the loneliness of others
  and understand their yearning for friends
Help me to sense the anxiety of others
  and respond to it with sensitivity
Help me to be aware of the fears of others
  and offer the love that casts out fear
Help me to know the pain of others
  and so minister relevantly to it

Amen

December 8

A Thought

As salt permeating the earth has its secret effect (Matthew 5:13), so must disciples influence the life of the world. So with light. As lights shining in the world, so must disciples "shine". For where there is salt or light, things will begin to happen. New life will begin to grow.

"I am the light of the world" (John 9:5). "Let your light so shine before men that they may see your good works and glorify your Father which is in heaven" (Matthew 5:16).

Light brings warmth: warmth creates life.

A Prayer

In a world often cold
  help me to offer warmth, O God
In a world often hard
  help me to ease the path of others
In a world often gloomy
  help me to generate joy
In a world often sad
  help me to offer comfort

                              Amen

December 9

A Thought

We are not prevented, if we are determined to do it, from going to "the far country" as the Prodigal Son did. The Father will wait for us.

The rich young ruler was free to say "No" and go away perhaps later to ruminate and possibly to return.

It is not the Divine way to overwhelm personality against one's will, but it is of the essence of the Divine will to long and to wait, in order, ultimately, to receive.

"There is joy in heaven over one sinner that repenteth."

A Prayer

Let heaven's arches ring
  and angels sing
    when I return, penitent
      to Your love
For to be dead, then alive
  lost and then found
    is an experience of blessing
For which I give thanks

                              Amen

December 10

A Thought

Justification (or spiritual turning-point) and sanctification (or spiritual growth) are not possible without the realities we cannot prove, but by which we live and on which we base all . . . that God was incarnate in Jesus Christ, that the risen Christ promised the living, active energy and presence of the Holy Spirit.

These are the fundamentals of our faith and we cannot treat them as if they were not true.

Love divine exists.
New life is offered.

A Prayer
Let there be light
* along my way*
Let there be love around me
* on the way*
Let there be life
* as the way unfolds*

Amen

December 11

A Thought

The Christian doctrine of forgiveness is of primary importance for it is the most therapeutic of all doctrines. An understanding of the meaning of forgiveness will give a balance to life that is crucial, and provide a perspective on life that is sound.

Life should not be gloomy with guilt, but glad because there is forgiveness. It is real! Believe it!

A Prayer

Make my life, O Lord
  a melody of grace
  a dance of joy
  a song of hope
  a vesper of peace

Amen

December 12

A Thought

Holy worldliness involves "involvement" *and* "distance". "Worldliness" is the involvement. "Holiness" implies distance. It is not the Christian's function to opt out of the world. As with Christ Himself, his only possible place is within it. It is the Christian's responsibility to realise the call to holiness and accept the true apartness involved. The recovery of apartness and, in that sense, holiness, must be a discipline for all who seek to grow in grace. It is easier to be "worldly" than to be "holy".

A Prayer

When tension fills my body
  grant me, O God, Your peace
Let peace, like a river, flow through me
  bringing relaxation, rest and regeneration
So may I be renewed in body and soul

Amen

December 13

A Thought

It is the claim of the Christian faith that the insight into life which came in Jesus Christ and comes through the power of the Spirit provides a true perspective on life and leads to balance and wholeness. The attainment of that true perspective must be the aim and prayer of the sanctified soul.

A Prayer

Make me to move quickly
  when obedience demands, O Lord
Help me to walk slowly
  when growth requires it
Let me take up enthusiastically
  new projects of grace
Keep me consistent
  in all I undertake
For You are constant and never change

Amen

December 14

A Thought

The words of Jesus to the two disciples who walked the Emmaus road were very strong! "O fools", He said, "and slow of heart to believe all that the prophets have spoken! Ought not Christ to have suffered these things?" To which the answer must be: "Yes, of course" for only thus, it seems, could He "enter His glory".

A Prayer
Lord, forgive me if
  my anger is unrighteous
  my envy is uncontrollable
  my jealousy is real
  my irritation is inexcusable
Give me rather the gentle graces
  through the power of Your Spirit

Amen

December 15

A Thought

There is plenty of room for divine eccentricity and

enthusiastic individualism in the service of the kingdom
(otherwise how can we ever be "fools for Christ's sake"?) but
beneath and around the life motivated by the Spirit, there is a
balance, an order, a harmony and a wholeness that speaks of
His presence.

A Prayer

You are my shepherd, O Lord
  I shall want nothing
You restore my soul
You lead me in right paths
Filled with Your love
I shall fear no evil
For You are with me
  Always

                              Amen

December 16

A Thought

Caution converted becomes commitment. Thomas'
declaration of belief on the receipt of the proof he requested,
becomes outstanding conviction to be remembered, for all
time, by his cry: "My Lord and my God!" (John 20:28). It is
a cry from the same level to the same level as was Mary
Magdalene's: "My Master" (John 20:16). Once the truth is
revealed, you can and must throw caution to the winds!

A Prayer

O Lord, make me bold
  in all I think
  in all I plan
  in all I do
So that I represent the faith
  I claim to hold
    with courage

                         Amen

December 17

A Thought

Grace reaches down into the very depths of the human struggle, which is a war in the soul between good and evil; a war between all that is on the side of good and is therefore uplifting, strengthening, inspiring, purifying and invigorating and all that belongs to evil – that which lowers, degrades, defiles, make less, reduces in spiritual stature. All these latter things are grace-less. "Love never does the grace-less thing" (I Corinthians 13:5, William Barclay).

A Prayer
If I forget You, O Lord
  forget not me
If I fail You, O Lord
  leave me not comfortless
If I lose You, O Lord
  lose not me
If my love is weak, O Lord
  still love me

Amen

December 18

A Thought

Goodness like so much in the spiritual area becomes less attainable the more we *try* to achieve it, for goodness is a product, not an aim. It is the result of the Spirit's work within us. It is most visible to others when we ourselves cannot see it. It has most effect on the world when we are not aware that we are proclaiming it.

A Prayer
When I look on the crowded world in my prayers
Help me, O God, not to be overwhelmed by its problems for
I cannot solve them all nor

Can I have significant influence on them
But enable me to see that
What I can give I must give
What I can influence, I must try to influence

Amen

December 19

A Thought

I once interviewed someone who had worked for 10 years in animal welfare. I asked her why. "It was to pay my debt to animals," she said.

"Debt?" I said.

"Yes," she replied. "I was beaten and battered by my parents as a young child, so I should have grown up unloving and unloved. But I had a dog, who loved me and whom I loved. That dog prevented me from losing the capacity to know and show love."

A Prayer

Oh Master, grant that I may never seek
so much to be consoled as to console
to be understood as to understand
to be loved as to love
with all my soul

Amen

(based on words by Sebastian Temple)

December 20

A Thought

You would expect that those who earnestly discussed questions of theology relating to the crucified and risen Christ on the road to Emmaus, would be aware of his presence. But they didn't recognise him. Theology by itself does not open eyes to the real presence of the Lord. So let us beware of

making academic discussion about Christ a substitute for
faith.

A Prayer
Lead me, Lord
  Lead me in Your righteousness
Make my way plain
  And grant me safety

                    Amen

December 21

A Thought

So subtle and insinuating are the forces of so-called
sophistication that, as with Pharoah's ever-hardening heart,
we fail to sense the diminution in our standards and find
ourselves sharing in attitudes to life, death and people that fall
short of our deeper desires and do not speak of our true
selves.

A Prayer
Prevent, O Lord
  the hardening of my heart
  with its
      loss of pity
        lack of sensitivity
          lessening love
Draw me with the cords of love
  and so increase
      my compassion
        my understanding
          my responses
  that I move through life
  reflecting the example of my Lord

                    Amen

December 22

A Thought

"When the soul has purified himself" writes St. Denis, a fifteenth-century mystic, "when she burns with the fire of charity, when she shines by reason of her virtues, God takes His pleasure greatly in her. He holds her familiarly like a fair spouse, clasping her, caressing her, embracing her and communicating His blessings to her, abundantly."

A Prayer
In widening circles, I bring to You, O Lord
  the family
    the community
      the nation
        the world
          and the church, militant and triumphant
Hold them all in Your hands, I pray

Amen

December 23

A Thought

Stars that have been followed with eagerness and enthusiasm have failed to lead to salvation. The belief that, first, education, then science, then psychology would provide the answers to all man's needs, lies crushed and broken.

The false pursuits go on, but the Christian remedy remains. "There's none but Christ can satisfy."

A Prayer
Into Your hands, O Lord
  I commit
    those who are ill
    those mentally troubled
    those nervously upset
    those anxious about tomorrow

those distressed about yesterday
Grant each of them Your peace

                 Amen

December 24

A Thought

Christ has no hands but our hands
   to do His work today
Christ has no feet but our feet
   to lead men in His way
Christ has no lips but our lips
   to tell men that He died
Christ has no help but our help
   to bring them to His side

A Prayer
Use me, O Lord
   as You will
     when . . .
       where . . .
         how . . .
Grant only that I shall be
   obedient to "the heavenly vision"
My promise I renew this holy Eve

                 Amen

December 25

A Thought

Follow the star, and find through it, like wise men of old, that you find your Lord. Find, in the holy Mary, a richness that enriches your whole life. Ponder the extra-ordinary self-giving of Joseph whose deeply spiritual intuition played such a part in making it possible for the holy child of Bethlehem to be "ours today".

A Prayer

O Holy Child of Bethlehem
  Descend to us, we pray
Cast out our sin and enter in
  Be born in us today
O come to us
  Abide with us
    Our Lord
      Immanuel
        God with us

Amen

(Phillips Brooks)

December 26

A Thought

Jürgen Moltmann, the German theologian, says that living in hope "is an experiment". He goes on: "Hoping is a risky matter, it can bring disappointment and surprise developments. To live in hope is a mark of the Christian."

We need a theology of hope today – and to take the risks involved.

A Prayer

It is never night
  if You are near, O Lord
It is never dark
  if Your light shines, O Lord
It is never bleak
  if Your warmth enfolds, O Lord

Amen

December 27

A Thought

It is hard to live and think and act as if "the things that are seen are temporal while the things that are not seen are eternal" (II Corinthians 4:18). This, in worldly terms, is the opposite of truth and an invitation to foolishness. The physical is, of course, the "real" to the world. The senses apprehend reality. To make the spiritual into reality is to fly in face of "the facts", to court disaster.

Yet to do just that is the instruction on the Christian's "map". His is a map of life determined by that perspective. Because of it, he will see the whole of life, its meaning, its pain, its joy and its happenings in a different way.

A Prayer

I need You every hour
  O gracious Lord
    The pressures I face are heavy
    The problems I meet are grievous
    The solutions I seek are elusive
    The peace I need is gone
Grant me Your presence
  and Your peace, I pray

                              Amen

December 28

A Thought

There are, in life, the things which we cannot change – like age, a physical limitation and similar hindrances with which we have to live. In such circumstances, we "learn therewith to be content" as Paul reminds us. But the real limitations we accept must not lead us to forget that what we can change, we should change, especially if it is limiting or unworthy.

Let us keep alive the true spirit of the rebel within us!

A Prayer

The weight of the world's needs weighs heavy on me, O God
  I see that starving child
    and I cry within

I hear the voice of the displaced person
  and from the security of my home, I worry
I read of war and violence, constantly
  and I feel the pain of those who suffer through it
Lord, give me always
  an understanding heart
  a compassionate mind and
  a loving soul
Where any of Your children are in need

Amen

December 29

A Thought

You may, in the eventide of life, say with Simeon that you can go on your journey in peace because your eyes have seen salvation. In the fullness of life you may join the crowds who spread their garments in the way of the Lord of life.

There is no fixed route to salvation and the health of the soul . . . though so many try to confine the Spirit by insisting that there is. What matters is that *we* find the way that leads to life.

A Prayer

May I give my heart to
  sympathy with the suffering, O Lord
May I give my mind to
  changing all that makes for suffering
May I give my strength to
  aiding the afflicted and helping the hurt

Amen

December 30

A Thought

Ben Travers, the 93-year old playwright, has decided on his epitaph. It will be: "This is where the real fun begins".

A Prayer

May hope spring eternal within me, O Lord, so that
    I never give up anyone as hope-less
    I never lose enthusiasm
    I never fail to be stimulated by the future
Thus, saved by hope, may I find life ever new

                    Amen

December 31

A Thought

"Do you see yonder shining Light?" asked Evangelist of Christian in *Pilgrim's Progress*. "I think I do" Christian said. "Then," said Evangelist, "keep that light in Your eye."

A Prayer

Day by Day
Dear Lord of Thee
Three things I pray
    To see Thee more clearly
    To love Thee more dearly and
    To follow Thee more nearly
        Day by Day

May I make this prayer my own
    Each day of the new year
And serve You as You deserve
    A day at a time

                    Amen

(The prayer referred to is attributed to St. Richard of Chichester)

Book References

July 3	In the Silence by Father Andrew (*Mowbray*)
July 31	A Moment of Time by Apa Pant (*Hodder & Stoughton*)
August 4	The Unconscious God by Viktor Frankl (*Hodder & Stoughton*)
August 15	Tensions by Harry Williams (*Mitchell Beazley*)
August 20	He is risen by Thomas Merton (*Argus*)
August 31	A Diary of Private Prayer by John Baillie (*Oxford University Press*)
September 8	Ways of the Spirit edited by Elizabeth Hamilton (*Darton, Longman & Todd*)
September 16	Guide to Hidden Springs by Mark Gibbard (*SCM Press*)
September 28	As a Man Thinketh by James Allen (*RHS Publications*)
October 15	Exploring Silence by Wendy Robinson (*SLG Press, Convent of the Incarnation, Fairacres, Oxford, England*)
October 26	Invitation to Pilgrimage by John Baillie (*Oxford University Press*) A Diary of Private Prayer by John Baillie (*Oxford University Press*)
November 9	Smouldering Fire by Martin Israel (*Hodder & Stoughton*)
December 4	Saint in the Slums by Cyril Davey (*Epworth*)

The New Testament (2 volumes) translated by William Barclay is published by Collins.